TRANSFORMATIVE DONOR ORGANIZING:
The Developing Theory and Practice

ISAAC LEV SZMONKO

solidaire

ORGANIZE
THE
RICH

Suggested citation: Szmonko, Isaac Lev. *Transformative Donor Organizing: The Developing Theory and Practice.* 1st ed., Solidaire Network, 2025.

® UNION CWA LABEL 5

Solidaire Network is a vibrant, intergenerational network of donor and funder organizers and movement leaders working toward social justice. Our vision of radical giving invites both donors and foundation staff to transform themselves and their relationship to power by resourcing frontline movements for the long term. **SolidaireNetwork.org**

Organize the Rich is a multimedia project sharing interviews, stories and analysis about what it means to organize the rich toward justice as part of multiracial working-class-led movements. **linktr.ee/OrganizeTheRich**

Contents

This isn't just about stopping authoritarianism. It's about making sure that when we win, what stands in its place is not the status quo of racism, wealth inequality, sexism and transphobia, but a real chance for a future where every human being lives with dignity, love and power.

Executive Summary

We live during a time of rising authoritarianism, climate crises, extreme wealth inequality and militarism. While billions flow into Right-wing organizing every year, progressive movements rooted in working-class communities and communities of color remain chronically under-resourced.

Traditional models of working with wealthy progressive people — centered on fundraising and light political education — are simply insufficient to meet the moment. We need to organize as many wealthy people as possible to give the majority of their wealth to grassroots power-building, to leverage their political and social capital in service of Left strategy and to organize other wealthy people to do the same.

This isn't just about stopping authoritarianism. It's about making sure that when we win, what stands in its place is not the status quo of racism, wealth inequality, sexism and transphobia, but a real chance for a future in which every human being lives with dignity, love and power. We need to deploy tens of billions of dollars over the next decade behind strategies that build power in working-class communities and communities of color, and build governing power for the Left. To do this, we need Transformative Donor Organizing.

A Transformative Donor Organizing approach creates rigorous and loving political homes where wealthy people can undergo deep personal and political transformation. It supports them to move from being passive allies to becoming lifelong revolutionary actors who see their own interests tied to the liberation of all people and commit their full resources, relationships and power to building a feminist, socialist, regenerative economy.

The methodology includes the following:

- **Long-term political homes** that nurture belonging, loving community, dignity and accountable relationships to grassroots movements

- **Transformative political education** that uses storytelling, open-ended inquiry, embodiment, care and radical honesty to change people and not just ideas. This education connects wealth accumulation to systemic violence, helps transform harmful socialization beliefs and patterns, creates a sense of having a stake in collective liberation and builds an understanding of movement visions and strategies.

- **Leadership development** that supports people to become strong organizers for wealth redistribution

- **Collective action,** including pooled or aligned giving, political advocacy and divestment campaigns

- **Spiritual and emotional work** that includes healing, personal and community transformation and the cultivation of a sense of deep purpose and commitment

- **Practical support** to create strategic multi-year giving plans, give in ways that help movements thrive, divest from the stock market and organize their families and wealth managers

Transformative Donor Organizing is not about perfecting donor behavior; it's about building the organizing infrastructure to unlock wealth and power for liberation movements, so we can create a different world. The question isn't *if* wealthy people can be powerful agents for liberatory change — it's whether we'll build the organizations powerful enough to make that transformation inevitable.

We *can* transform segments of the owning class into powerful comrades — not just for their money, but for their relationships, skills and lifelong commitment to liberation. We hope this essay is a contribution toward just that.

ONE

Toward a Transformative Donor Organizing Approach

We need highly aligned segments of the owning classes to contribute not just their financial resources, but also their political capital, relationships, organizing capacities and other skills to a broader Left strategy for structural change.

F or as long as organizing for societal change has existed, movements have worked to attract financial and political support from wealthy people, and wealthy people have been a direct part of efforts for change — from the reactionary to the revolutionary.

In the US, the social justice movements of the 1960s and 1970s inspired new approaches to what became called "donor organizing."[1] These efforts tried to build more support for the radical movements of the times through peer-to-peer organizing and organization-building among wealthy people. They sought to answer a key question: *Could creating a political home specifically for wealthy progressives create significant advances in efforts to resource social justice movements?* Fifty years later, after the rise and fall of many donor networks and philanthropic organizations, we can definitively answer "yes" to that question.

However, after decades of neoliberalism, with devastating racialized wealth inequality, tremendous state violence and a global owning class[2] continuing to ravage poor and working-class communities and the planet itself, this question is far too small.

We exist in a time when marginalized communities and democracy itself are being successfully scapegoated for the brutal economic and social impacts of

---

1   Michael Gast and others, like former Resource Generation Executive Director Iimay Ho, have pushed us to give up the term "donor organizing" when what we mean is organizing rich people, both because it makes invisible the fact that most movement donors are poor or working class and because it creates an identity that is specifically and only around the identity of being a "donor," when we are actually trying to get progressive wealthy people to organize consciously and more broadly from their class position. Since "donor organizing" is a widely used term, we'll be using it in this essay, even though what we really mean is organizing progressive people who either are wealthy themselves or belong to wealthy families whom they can influence.

2   The term "owning class" refers to people who own significant amounts of wealth and who primarily derive income from ownership of land, businesses, stocks and other forms of capital, instead of from wages or salaries. Even those who start off being wealthy through high wages most often become a part of this owning class through investing. In this essay, we will use "wealthy" and "owning class" mostly interchangeably.

racial capitalism. This has led to a global rise in reactionary nationalism and authoritarianism that even further concentrates wealth and power for the owning class. Climate disasters are forcing more people to flee their homes, and political leaders are responding with increased militarism, increasing human displacement, suffering and death. When that coerced migration collides with nationalism, the seeds for popular support for fascism get watered even more.

So what now? Given these overlapping and escalating crises, what's the significance of donor organizing today? What responsibility do people with wealth have in the fight for our future? Why should the Left prioritize organizing wealthy people as a part of power-building for liberation?

Our Vision

Solidaire believes we need a radical restructuring of our political, economic and social systems that democratizes both power and resources toward new systems that center human needs in sustainable ways. We believe that to achieve that transformation, we need both small and large-scale progressive organizations rooted in the multiracial working class that build leadership and collective power for racial, economic, gender and climate justice. And we believe we need these organizations to be consistently well-funded to contest with the billions of dollars that are poured into Right-wing and neoliberal organizations and candidates every year.

While the multiracial working class needs to be organized at scale, we also need highly aligned segments of the owning class to contribute not just their financial resources, but also their political capital, relationships, organizing capacities and other skills to a broader Left strategy for structural change.

To make this vision possible, we need independent organizations that are political homes to bring in and develop progressive wealthy people with a rigorous organizing approach.

We believe investing in the strength of both of these types of organizations, as part of a broad- based working-class-led united front, is crucial to building Left governing power and the society of our dreams.[3]

Core Thesis

At Solidaire, we are attempting to organize and strengthen this movement-aligned base of donor members with an approach we're calling Transformative Donor Organizing.

The central thesis of a Transformative Donor Organizing approach is that it is possible, desirable and worth the effort to transform some wealthy people into lifelong revolutionary actors who see their own interests tied to the liberation of all people. With strong support, they will commit themselves to the radical restructuring of our political economy, the abolition of racial and gendered capitalism and the establishment of a feminist, socialist, regenerative economy. Though not everyone involved will become fully aligned in that way, many will move significantly toward this direction and bring wealth and power along with them.

We believe this approach is the best way to meet our goal of organizing wealthy donors to:

1. Give very significant amounts of their wealth to social justice movements over the course of their lives, with the majority going to working-class power-building

---

3   According to Grassroots Power Project and Grassroots Power Program, building Left governing power "means both controlling the government as it is and creating new systems and structures of governance. ... To win governing power, we need the capacity to design, drive demand for, legislate, enforce and defend a structural reform agenda that serves the interests of the multiracial working class. ... This requires us to reshape the structure of the government itself, so that it can advance democratic control, redistribution, and reparation" (*Governing Power* [2023]).

2. Give in ways that powerfully resource and flank social justice movements, and meaningfully intervene in harmful power dynamics, including yielding or sharing power over some decision-making

3. Follow the leadership of and keep funding movements, even when disagreement, conflict or fear arises, or when organizations experience failure or very difficult transitions

4. Use their full power as connected and skilled political actors to lend power to grassroots campaigns

5. Become skilled donor organizers and philanthropic organizers who can help bring more wealthy people into our movements and free up significantly more capital and aligned political action for movements than we will ever find in our own donor network memberships

Transformative Donor Organizing is a departure from most existing models of working with progressive wealthy people. It posits that *you can't fundraise or educate someone into transformation*. Instead, wealthy people need true political homes to practice accountability, move toward wealth redistribution, leverage their political connections and navigate difficult family and peer organizing that expands resources for social justice movements.

Our Challenge

The vast majority of existing approaches to working with progressive wealthy people can't accomplish either well-funded working-class organizations *or* political and organizing homes for the owning class.

While many progressive organizations use the term "donor organizing" to describe how they engage wealthy people, they are usually describing some combination of relational fundraising,[4] light political education and shallow community-building.

There are three main versions of what "donor organizing" looks like (these will be addressed more deeply in the "Lineage" section):

1. **Donor-centered education and services.** There are donor organizing networks within philanthropy that prioritize the comfort, needs and desires of wealthy people over the goals of wealth redistribution and societal transformation. In this version, there is little accountability to or alignment with progressive multiracial working-class movements.

2. **Multiracial working-class organizations and alliances.** There is a Left version of donor organizing that engages donors or potential donors of particular organizations or alliances in relational fundraising and some political education, but is not designed to offer a substantive political home for the rich.

3. **Majority-white, multi-class organizations.** Even organizations that are not strictly working-class focused, and have bases that include a significant number of wealthy people, rarely have the desire, skills or capacity to meaningfully engage their wealthy members in class-conscious ways — let alone support them to redistribute wealth or organize wealthy people into movement in a way that's deeply aligned with working-class interests.

For the purposes of this essay, donor organizing goes beyond relational fundraising, donor services and education. Instead, donors become active members of an organization that provides the infrastructure to mobilize them to take

---

4   Michael Kiragu explains: "Transactional fundraising involves focusing on short-term, one-off donations, and treating donors as sources of immediate revenue. This approach tends to prioritize financial transactions and may not take into account the donor's long-term engagement or commitment to the organization. In contrast, relational fundraising centers around building and nurturing long-term, mutually beneficial relationships with donors. It recognizes that donors are more than just cheque books; they are partners in a shared mission." ("The Power of Relationships: Why Non-profit Fundraisers Need to Adopt a Relational Approach," LinkedIn, October 25, 2023).

consistent individual and collective action within a shared strategy, while growing their skills, leadership and sense of belonging.

Transformative Donor Organizing is a specific approach to donor organizing that takes lessons from past donor organizing models and progressive organizing of privileged communities. It also applies the key tenets of the Transformative Organizing model developed by the social movement Left to build power in working-class communities of color.

TWO

Lineage: The Origins of Our Transformative Donor Organizing Approach

Without a rigorous political home, most progressive wealthy people will remain out of reach, give to "false solutions" or only ever give a tiny fraction of their wealth to movements.

S olidaire's approach to Transformative Donor Organizing is informed by several organizing lineages in the US:

1. Transformative Organizing in the social movement Left, focused on building bases and power in working-class communities of color

2. Organizing of communities with some positional privilege and power that is trying to align with working-class progressive organizing

3. Progressive donor and funder organizing

In this section, we'll explore how these traditions shape our approach to Transformative Donor Organizing, while identifying where we need to break from past assumptions or practices to build an aligned base of wealthy people who are both major donors and effective organizers for Left structural change.

Lineage 1: Social Movement Left and Transformative Organizing

Some of Solidaire's greatest political influences in the US are organizations that are sometimes called the "social movement Left" — broadly, anti-capitalists who seek to bring forward a Left, anti-racist and feminist alternative to racial and gendered capitalism by building power in white working-class communities and communities of color through a Transformative Organizing approach.[5]

Transformative Organizing is a methodology for building multiracial working-class power through base-building and movement-building to challenge

---

5 Eric Mann, who at the time was at the Labor Community Strategy Center (LCSC), first articulated the Transformative Organizing model in the publication *Weaving the Threads* ("Transformative Organizing," 17, no. 2, [Fall 2010], https://www.reimaginerpe.org/17-2/mann). For many years, LCSC ran the National School for Strategic Organizing, where young leaders, mostly organizers of color, were trained to execute this model. Many leaders of transformative Left organizing today have either themselves been trained by this program or have been trained by people who come from that lineage. Since then, organizations like Right to the City Alliance, Grassroots Global Justice Alliance and Movement for Black Lives have been further documenting the model, practicing it and continuing to train organizers in it.

both the Right wing and neoliberalism. The model seeks to ensure that a multiracial working-class front is at the center of broader forces that can effectively change living conditions for working-class people, expand democracy and democratic institutions and lay the foundation for broader social transformation.

Transformative Organizing is:

1. **Ideologically Left.** Transformative Organizing explicitly seeks to end racial and gendered capitalism, imperialism, heteropatriarchy and colonization, and build systemic alternatives based on anti-racist, feminist and regenerative policies and practices.[6] Strategy and tactics are shaped not just to win short-term material gains but to do so in a way that advances these visions and goals.

2. **Strategically focused on the leadership of oppressed classes.** It builds and supports the "leadership of society's most exploited, oppressed, and strategically placed classes and races" through base-building, leadership development and campaigns in mass-based organizations.[7]

3. **Counter-hegemonic in its campaigns and demands.**[8] Transformative Organizing aims to wage campaigns that shift meaningful power and resources toward working-class communities and communities of color, while shifting the dominant narratives and culture that uphold systems of domination. It pushes Left ideas into the mainstream. Some campaign examples include "Housing is a human right" and the campaign for universal healthcare, which oppose the dominant belief that the market

---

6   For more information on the vision, see Right to the City and Grassroots Global Justice Alliance's forthcoming document and School on Transformative Organizing.

7   Mann, "Transformative Organizing." The Transformative Organizing model doesn't follow a shallow identity politic model that assumes that people who are most exploited are already leaders because of their experiences of oppression, but instead assumes that their experiential knowledge of how systems of oppression operate and their material interest in a radically different system provide a good starting point for conscious development into Left leadership.

8   "Hegemony" is the set of ideas, beliefs and norms that the ruling class uses to persuade people to consent to their own domination. Counter-hegemonic demands are those that intentionally break with those ways of thinking to attempt to create a new common sense.

should control access to housing and healthcare. These campaigns also create conditions for eviction moratoriums, rent control and expanded Medicaid.

4. **Transformative at the individual, interpersonal and systemic levels.** Transformative Organizing aims to transform both the organizer and the people being organized as it transforms the world. Rooted in the understanding that we are all shaped by ideologies serving racial and gendered capitalism, Transformative Organizing aims to develop revolutionary leaders by reshaping internalized oppression and superiority, as well as capitalist values like individualism, competition and passivity. Similarly, the Transformative Organizing model understands that oppression causes trauma at the personal, community and systemic levels, and intentionally includes practices of well-being and healing — such as staff health benefits and meditative, somatic, spiritual or cultural healing spaces — as part of the organizing work. The Transformative Organizing approach draws from Marta Harnecker and other Latin American socialists by using the concept of social protagonism — the transformation of people who are being acted upon by systems and forces that seem outside of their control into conscious changemakers who are collaboratively, actively and strategically shaping the reality they live in.[9] This transformation requires creating spaces for people to codevelop and carry out political projects, build collective ownership and a shared political identity, and participate in shaping the organization's direction and governance.

5. **Oriented toward movement-building and alliance-building.** Organizations practicing Transformative Organizing spend significant time and energy building political alignment, trust, shared strategy and

---

9   LeftRoots explains, "We understand protagonism to be the democratic engagement that builds our individual and collective capacities for transformative change and, in doing so, combats our fundamental alienation from the means of production, from the products of our labor, from each other, and from ourselves" (*LeftRoots' Case Study on Left Organizational Culture* [n.d.], https://dusk.leftroots.net/resources/LeftRoots%20Org%20Culture% 20Case%20Study.pdf).

shared work across and beyond the social movement Left.[10] This shared work includes building multiracial and multi-class coalitions and other strategic allies — forces inside and outside the US that share a common strategic orientation and long-term vision, even if they organize different membership bases or organize inside other sectors. A front of strategic allies is sometimes called a historic bloc, an alignment of multiple social forces that understands itself to have both shared interest and identity in opposition to the status quo and in support of alternatives.[11]

A Transformative <u>Donor</u> Organizing approach shares most of these tenets, with a focus on organizing wealthy people to align with the Left leadership developed in working-class communities and communities of color and to step into a rightful place in the historic bloc. Many of the barriers to success in building this alignment come from the socialization wealthy people have into harmful ways of being, which we'll discuss more later. However, barriers also come out of the cultural tendencies of grassroots movements, including the social movement Left.

The dominant view within Left grassroots movements is that rich progressive people should fund movements but are not integral parts of them, especially if they are white. This view stems from both a strategic assessment that the most important revolutionary forces are working-class people of color and a constant pressing need for resources,[12] which often leads those in movements to priori-

---

10 Rising Majority is the latest example of this, but other alliances and their member organizations (such as Right to the City Alliance, Grassroots Global Justice Alliance, United We Dream, Grassroots Asians Rising, Showing Up for Racial Justice, Movement for Black Lives and Working Families Party) have been engaged in this for many years.

11 From a forthcoming document on Transformative Organizing by Right to the City Alliance and Grassroots Global Justice Alliance.

12 In the last decade, with surging inequality, Left grassroots movements have only become more dependent on a smaller number of wealthy supporters and foundations. Fewer organizations have a broad cross-class base of donors who can insulate them from the roller coaster that can be funding from the rich. This is a problem that is in part due to the decrease in support for and understanding of grassroots fundraising, especially with the closing of the Grassroots Institute for Fundraising Training (GIFT) in 2020. Efforts to train up a new generation of grassroots fundraisers from groups such as Resource Organizing Project, Democratizing Philanthropy Project, Wealth Reclamation Academy of Practitioners, Securing The Roots and Donor Organizer Hub are more important than ever.

tize mostly transactional — and sometimes relational — fundraising. However, this perspective is often heavily informed by trauma responses to racism, classism and other oppressions that can limit our collective vision.

In his article "Building Resilient Organizations," Working Families Party National Director Maurice Mitchell articulates a common tendency of neoliberal identity politics within Left movements, in which "identity is evidence of some intrinsic ideological or strategic legitimacy. Marginalized identity is deployed as a conveyor of a strategic truth that must simply be accepted. Likewise, historically privileged identities are essentialized, flattened, and frequently — for better or worse — dismissed."[13]

This tendency is exacerbated by the fact that many people who have liberatory visions of society feel some combination hate for rich people, discomfort around rich people and/or fear of rich people. Some have had little experience with actual wealthy people and instead have interacted in harmful ways with their middle agents (cops, social workers, building managers, prison guards, teachers, bank workers, immigration agents, the military, program officers, etc.).

Those who have interacted with wealthy people have often experienced direct exploitation or other material harm, and have almost always been on the receiving end of harmful owning-class behavioral patterns, including from donors to their organizations. There is abundant unhealed trauma and protective anger from these interactions and, for many, from the general experiences of class oppression while growing up.

This orientation to the rich is not limited to working-class people and is how we frequently see owning-class people treat each other. Similarly to dynamics in white anti-racist organizing, owning-class progressive people can have the harmful tendencies of trying to "be the best wealthy person" or connecting with working-class people by critiquing and distancing from other wealthy

---

13 Maurice Mitchell, "Building Resilient Organizations," *The Forge*, November 29, 2022, https://forgeorganizing.org/article/building-resilient-organizations.

people instead of providing a supportive pathway for the wealthy person's development and meaningful participation. We often see wealthy people who are a part of progressive or Left movements try to hide their wealth to fit in or avoid accountability around money, sometimes leaning into oppressed aspects of their identity. These behaviors may be driven by shame, projection and a fear of not belonging.

With all of these class dynamics, it is difficult for many people on the Left to imagine that we can and should intentionally organize wealthy people to be transformative leaders who have specific but crucial roles to play. While many organizations do their best to engage in relational fundraising, most organizations and people in Left movements have attempted to have as little as possible to do with wealthy donors, while getting as much as possible of their money — seeing them as outside of the sphere of movement or organizing and more like annoying ATMs that one has to persuade to release the cash so others can "do the real work."

The model of only "organizing" wealthy people through relational fundraising, without a political home, leaves tremendous financial and human resources on the table. It allows wealthy donors to remain solo players who are not accountable to a larger political vision or community. Without a rigorous political home, most progressive wealthy people will remain out of reach, give to "false solutions" or only ever give a tiny fraction of their wealth to movements.[14]

Transformative Donor Organizing posits that this orientation toward wealthy people is reactive, unstrategic and overly pessimistic. We are routinely discarding or underinvesting in people who could bring significant financial and political power into movements solely because of their socialization into dominant, supremacist and entitled behavior. We instead propose that the Left

---

14   The term "false solutions" comes out of the climate justice movement and addresses the dynamic in which corporations, governments and nongovernmental organizations propose and implement supposed "solutions" to the problems caused by racial capitalism with methods that actually reinforce the harmful power dynamics and exploitation of racial capitalism.

should seek to break off a small, organizable segment of the owning class who can transform and become leaders around wealth redistribution as part of multiracial, working-class-centered, liberatory movements. We must do so with the full understanding that you can't lead when you're mired in guilt and shame and not grounded in your own sense of dignity and purpose.

To be clear, we don't believe that most working-class organizations should set themselves up for Transformative Donor Organizing (though most would benefit from more relational fundraising approaches).

Instead, we encourage leaders from working-class organizations to politically invest in organizations (like Solidaire) that are attempting to organize segments of the owning class–not just as places to seek resources, but as aligned strategic organizing that will free up more resources for grassroots movements as a whole.

This collaboration will require both a move away from a limited "ally" model and a real shift to stop thinking of all wealthy people as targets, obstacles or people to hustle.

Lineage 2: "Mutual Interest," "Collective Liberation" and "Joint Struggle" Organizing Approaches with Privileged Communities

Another important lineage comes from organizations that develop aligned strategic fighting forces from more privileged communities as important parts of revolutionary struggle — even as they agree that working-class communities of color are where most organizing and financial resources need to focus. These organizations build Left politics and power in multiracial but majority-white communities, focusing on constituencies such as white working-class people, queer and trans people, women or Jewish people; those focused on specific issues like climate change; or geographic communities that are key to building progressive electoral power.[15] Many of these organizations follow the organizing modalities of Transformative Organizing, and partner directly with mass-based organizations that are rooted in working-class communities of color.

Importantly, these organizations do not follow a traditional "ally" model and instead have an orientation that is described as "collective liberation," "mutual interest" or "joint struggle." Though they believe that working-class communities of color need to be the primary visionary and strategic leadership of revolutionary struggle, they seek to develop significant leadership capacities among their constituencies and organize people to understand and move from their own self-interest in radical structural change. They take this approach partly because of an assessment that we need to build majoritarian power that includes some privileged communities and partly out of a deep-seated belief that all of us really do benefit from a radical change in society, including those of us who receive some material and psychological benefits from the current system.

These organizations seek to cultivate something different from the ally model, which assumes that people don't have their own interest in ending racial capitalism. The ally approach often produces a variety of problems, including passivity, political underdevelopment, tokenism, subservience, saviorism/martyrdom and shallow commitment. These organizations may include wealthy people within their constituencies but rarely develop class consciousness among them, support significant wealth redistribution, move significant resources outside of their own fundraising or build skills for organizing other wealthy and powerful people.

Some may choose to develop a Transformative Donor Organizing approach if it aligns with their mission; others may prefer strategic partnerships with aligned donor organizations that support their members' growth as leaders for wealth redistribution.

---

15 Some examples include Jewish Voice for Peace and Jews for Racial and Economic Justice (Jews); Sunrise Movement (climate justice); Rural Organizing Project, Down Home North Carolina and Kentuckians for the Commonwealth (majority-white but multiracial working class); and Showing Up for Racial Justice (cross-class white people with focus on working-class white people and targeted electoral work).

Lineage 3: Progressive Donor and Funder Organizing

Our organizing lineage at Solidaire intertwines with both earlier-described approaches, as well as with the history of progressive philanthropy organizations.

Philanthropic networks and service organizations have ranged in approaches from donor services to donor education, but rarely practice donor organizing.

In **donor service organizations**, wealthy people pay to be members or make donations in exchange for a set of services that support their giving in some way — such as donor advising or strategic briefings. These organizations often have some educational programming, but members are treated mostly like clients.

Organizations oriented toward **donor education** seek to impact donors' behavior primarily through hosting events and seminars during which donors learn about specific topics related to their giving from experts in the field. Many organizations that use the term "donor organizing" actually stop here with donor education.

The great majority of philanthropic organizations and donor networks center wealthy people's needs and comfort, have shallow donor engagement models and/or have little to no accountability to grassroots movements. Some focus on getting a small percentage of wealthy people's resources toward specific causes, like electoral organizing, while offering some surface-level political education or a shallow sense of belonging. Other groups are set up to attract wealthy people by offering cultural capital — they are interesting spaces where the main draw is the chance to socialize with other powerful people while hearing from "innovators" and being lauded for your efforts. Some groups claim to be values-neutral and view all philanthropy as positive, while bringing wealthy people together to talk about the nuts and bolts of philanthropy or centrist giving, such as the funding of social services.

There are also powerful models of donor engagement that offer transformative political education, but don't provide a political home, deeper leadership development or ongoing collective action. The Giving Project Network, Grassroots International's delegations, the Thousand Currents Academy and some of the cohorts offered by our donor advisor/money coach friends are some examples.[16]

When we talk about **donor organizing**, we are referring to roots that go back to the early 80s and the work of Christopher and Anne Ellinger, along with many others in the social justice philanthropy ecosystem. The term "donor organizing" was meant to shift "thinking away from seeing donors simply as people who gave money, to seeing donors as people to fully engage as part of the community working for change."[17] Here are the four main principles, as described by the Ellingers:

1. Hear the personal stories of role models (and eventually, to share their own stories).

2. Join a network or support group with like-minded people supporting and challenging continued growth.

3. Receive ongoing support to thoughtfully prepare three important planning documents: (a) an estate plan, (b) a long-term giving plan, (c) and a social investment plan.

4. Get personal coaching and/or professional support to address their individual needs.

For the purposes of this essay, and expanding beyond the Ellingers' model, "donor organizing" goes beyond fundraising, services and education. Donors become active members of an organization that provides infrastructure to mo-

---

16 "Home," Giving Project Network, accessed August 4, 2025, https://www.givingprojects.org; "How Much Is Really Enough?," Align Your Wealth with Iris Brilliant, accessed August 4, 2025, https://www.irisbrilliant.com/overcoming.

17 This quote is from Christopher and Anne Ellinger's unpublished manuscript "Acting in the World—and on Stage." Christopher and Anne Ellinger (formerly Christopher Mogil and Anne Slepian) are longtime leaders in the world of progressive donor organizing. They popularized the term "donor organizing," developed the practice of donor advising in the 80s and 90s, cowrote the book *We Gave Away a Fortune*, cofounded organizations such as More Than Money and Bolder Giving, and have been central to developing the theory and practice of this work.

bil ze them to take consistent individual and collective action within a shared strategy, while growing their skills and leadership.

While different organizations have attempted donor organizing, Resource Generation (RG) has led the way in the development of a Transformative Donor Organizing model through its work organizing young people (ages 18-35) with wealth.

RG was founded in 1998 by a group of wealthy people and social justice philanthropy organizations in the Boston area. The organization grew out of previous efforts to help young, wealthy inheritors move money to and engage in the radical organizing and Left efforts of the times. RG borrowed from common community organizing strategies, such as chapter and membership models, base-building through peer-to-peer outreach, political education, organizing and leadership trainings, and campaigns — all adapted for its unique constituency.

There are many more organizations and individuals who have influenced the practice and development of donor organizing. A truly cross-class multiracial crew of activists, organizers, philanthropy professionals and wealthy progressives contributed to the theory and practice of this approach. We are indebted to their efforts. For more on this history, check out Organize the Rich, a project of Solidaire that documents stories and lessons from the last 50 years of this work.[18]

18　"Home," Organize the Rich, accessed August 4, 2025, https://organizetherich.substack.com.

THREE

Applying a Transformative Organizing Model to Donor Organizing

We will likely organize only a small portion of the owning class to voluntarily redistribute resources and power. The goal is to organize enough wealthy people to support movements that can win nonvoluntary redistribution measures (such as land reform and taxes) and transform our current systems to various forms of political and economic democracy.

T his section articulates several of the complications and tensions in applying a Transformative Organizing model, originally designed to center working-class people of color, to the wealthy and largely white constituency of the owning class.

Material Interest?

One core tenet of Transformative Organizing is building leadership among those with the greatest material interest in radical change.

There are two interlocking parts to this idea: 1) that people with the greatest material interest in a radically different system have the most reasons to fight in long-term, committed ways for that different world and can be organized en masse to do so and 2) that the visions and solutions from conscious organizers who come from the most exploited communities will have the most liberatory potential for everyone.

In contrast, the owning class is understood to have material interests that are aligned with racial capitalism, which has created the conditions for them to accumulate significant wealth, as well as economic, cultural and political power.

For this reason, models of organizing that focus on supporting wealthy people to identify their self-interest (and not just allyship or charity) in radical structural change have generally been based on the following assumptions:

1. We will likely organize only a small portion of the owning class to voluntarily redistribute resources and power. The goal is to organize enough wealthy people to support movements that can win nonvoluntary redistribution measures (such as land reform and taxes) and transform our current systems to various forms of political and economic democracy.

2. Therefore, practitioners of these models focus on helping owning-class people understand that while they materially benefit, there are significant

social, psychological, emotional and spiritual costs of both living in such an unequal society and knowing that your wealth has been accumulated and maintained through violence and exploitation.

3. Those practitioners then invite wealthy people into a mutually liberatory path of deep solidarity with Left movements.

This logic is increasingly relevant as wealthy people face — and can't escape — the material consequences of our political economy, from climate change to rising authoritarianism. We can assume these impacts will result in more wealthy people becoming open to fighting for a different future. Some organizations have also found that people of color, young people, women, Jews and queer and trans people who have wealth may more easily see how their liberation connects with everyone's ability to thrive.[19]

Multiple Centers and Collective Accountability

To develop wealthy people into powerful leaders for wealth redistribution within multiracial working-class movements, we must navigate multiple centers.

On the one hand, a Transformative Donor Organizing model agrees with the precepts that "society's most exploited, oppressed and strategically placed classes and races" must be at the forefront of radical structural change and that the organizing of wealthy people must be primarily in service of building power in those communities.[20]

On the other hand, it posits that wealthy people can and should have Left political homes; be politically developed; be supported to be organizers, leaders and "protagonists" for radical change both in their own communities and in

---

19 When you scratch under the surface of even white, middle-aged, cisgender and straight people in Left donor organizing, you usually find close loved ones who are directly targeted by systems of oppression.

20 Mann, "Transformative Organizing."

appropriate ways as a part of multiracial cross-class struggle; and experience their own liberation and transformation in this work.

Traditional models of donor organizing lean sharply toward one or the other of these centers in ways that either fail to truly support movements or produce short-term financial gains for movements while creating or exacerbating a boom-bust funding cycle. All the while, such models fail to develop members of the owning class who are willing to use their positional power accountably for progressive gains.

A Transformative Donor Organizing organization must stay rooted in and accountable to the politics, strategy, vision and leadership of Left movements building power in working-class communities and communities of color. We must continuously develop our own organizational political compass and clarity about the forces we are aligned with and how to build their power over time, and enroll members in those visions, politics and practices.

Organizations can collectivize donors' accountability to progressive working-class-led movements by embedding them within an accountability structure that aligns with movement goals. This requires that organizations practicing Transformative Donor Organizing identify and build relationships with the movement leadership and grassroots organizations with whom they are most closely aligned on political vision and strategy.

Some examples of collectivized donor accountability include:

1. Creating pooled funding of movements that is directed or advised by movement leaders

2. Organizing and advising donors to give directly to movement organizations

3. Building wealthy people's political alignment with the vision, goals and strategy of movement partners to inform giving and organizing

4. Organizing donors' political action/advocacy in alignment or direct coordination with specific campaigns, projects or efforts of movement partners

While each of these types of accountability is important, for a Transformative Donor Organizing organization, the broader accountability to working-class movements must be about claiming and continuing to develop the organization's ability to lead wealthy people to become lifelong committed parts of movement: bringing their full financial resources, their networks, their time, their passion and their skills. *We need to move beyond a shallow sense of one-sided accountability that is focused on the short-term, transactional resource hustle.* Fundraising is crucial, but we need to be very careful that an overemphasis on fundraising doesn't keep us from doing the work that shifts people out of incremental giving into wealth redistribution for liberation.

A Transformative Donor Organizing organization can facilitate closer relationships with movement in a way that is very different from an individual fundraising relationship, in which the power dynamic of financial need on the one hand and unearned power on the other is always interfering with authenticity and a sense of truly being in it together. *Organizations for wealthy people, if trusted, are able to facilitate relationships with working-class movements that are based on shared vision and strategy.* This can allow for more honesty and therefore deeper connection, while giving wealthy people practice sharing power and learning to listen deeply and value the wisdom of people who have had very different life experiences and who have been deeply harmed by other people's wealth accumulation.

These types of trusting relationships can create or amplify wealthy people's deep, heartfelt yearning for a different world. That is the stuff that moves mountains. Mountains of money, yes, but it also gives the type of inspiration that supports wealthy people to find appropriate places for their biggest, bravest leadership in coordination with movement partners toward an aligned vision and strategy.

FOUR

What Is to Be Transformed?

Transformative Donor Organizing seeks to move wealthy people away from seeking security, health, well-being, purpose, community, love, joy and pleasure in ways that require hoarding wealth and are enacted through structural and state violence. Instead, Transformative Donor Organizing moves them toward internalizing and embodying an understanding that the true "bread and roses" are to be found in a radically restructured, liberatory society, which they can help create.

With any wealthy person, there are specific aspects of transformation that require attention:

- **Countering hegemonic cultural norms.** These are the beliefs and ways of being that are created to sustain racial capitalism and are based in Western, Christian, patriarchal, white and American dominance. They manifest in personal ways of being (such as individualism, independence, competition and passivity), as well as broader political frameworks (such as rights-based libertarianism or American exceptionalism) that are counter to Left strategy and vision. All of these tendencies can harm collective projects. In place of these beliefs, Transformative Organizing seeks to create leadership that centers collectivity, collaboration, interdependence and protagonism, and a political framework that is internationalist, anti-imperialist and based in our collective human rights but also our responsibilities to each other.

- **Shifting wealthy people's understanding of self-interest.** Transformative Donor Organizing seeks to move wealthy people away from seeking security, health, well-being, purpose, community, love, joy and pleasure in ways that require hoarding wealth and are enacted through structural and state violence. Instead, Transformative Donor Organizing moves them toward internalizing and embodying an understanding that the true "bread and roses" are to be found in a radically restructured, liberatory society, which they can help create.[21]

- **Developing "right relationship to power."** Such a relationship centers sacredness, dignity, reciprocity, mutual responsibility, healing

---

21 The phrase "bread and roses," has contested origins but it is widely associated with women laborers who were on strike in the textile industry in 1912 and with the women's suffragette movement of the same time. Since then, the phrase bread and roses has been used as a rallying cry for worker rights and social justice movements to demand both material needs (bread) and the right to beauty, leisure, dignity and good working conditions (roses).

and sustainability and helps wealthy people develop centered accountability.

- **Healing trauma and countering internalized oppression and superiority.** This work is necessary so that all people can lead in liberatory ways toward a liberatory future.

Countering Hegemonic Cultural Norms

This work is not easy and it is not quick. Wealthy people's lives are usually very removed, in a day-to-day way, from working-class people who are not being paid to serve them. From that perspective, it is challenging for wealthy people to be able to truly imagine their lives as interdependent or intertwined with the lives of working-class people. The transformation we seek requires wealthy people to be willing and able to face the ways their wealth was extracted from these communities, and then learn how to relate to that truth without avoidance, defensiveness, guilt or shame, instead finding a sense of dignity, commitment and joy in repair by learning how to relate very differently.

To enable this, Transformative Donor Organizing seeks to transform the ways of being and ideas based in owning-class culture and white supremacy culture that are both more prominent in wealthy people and specifically impede the types of reflection and action we need wealthy people to take to fully and powerfully be a part of liberatory movements.

Building off of Tema Okun's work, I've written extensively about specific white supremacy culture patterns in wealthy donors (and not only white ones!), as well as some "antidotes."[22] Examples include patterns of perfectionism, a warped sense of urgency, defensiveness and fear of open conflict, valuing quantity over quality, worship of the written word, the thinking that there is "only one right way," paternalism, either-or thinking, the hoarding of money and

---

22   Isaac Lev Szmonko, "White Supremacy Culture As Wealthy Donors," n.d., https://bit.ly/whitesupremacydonors.

power, individualism, entitlement, the assumption of a right to comfort and a practiced lack of accountability.

Supporting people to move away from the approaches and behaviors that uphold domination into new ways of being that move toward liberation is one integral part of a Transformative Donor Organizing model. Importantly, though, the "transformative" part is realized when the new ways of being become integrated parts of a sense of self that acts in integrity with one's own values and desires, versus being motivated by a fear of getting it wrong, being "bad" or not belonging. Organizing that supports this internal motivation to grow is what produces long-lasting change.

Shifting Wealthy People's Understanding of Self-interest

Among wealthy people who have both redistributed significant resources and taken on leadership roles as donor organizers, there is a deep longing for a fundamentally different world. These individuals often struggle intensely with the discrepancy between their resources and relative safety, and others' fight to survive or barely get by. They come to understand that the war, policing, borders and exploitation that contradict their values exist precisely to ensure that people like them can accumulate wealth and power — and they want something different.

Beyond this recognition, they develop a deeper sense of their own stake in collective liberation. They see how current systems of racism, capitalism, colonialism and heteropatriarchy have harmed themselves and their families. For some, these harms are obvious: they or their families have escaped war or genocide, they continue to face racism, patriarchy or transphobia, or their families still live in poverty despite their wealth.

Even white, Christian, able-bodied straight men from multigenerational wealth can recognize how these systems harm them. They see that wealth brings deep separateness — alienation from and fear of other people. They struggle with building resilience or experiencing genuine interdependence. They worry about how much wealth to hold or pass to their children precisely because we live in a vastly unequal society that doesn't guarantee basic needs. They recognize how they and their families have had to suppress parts of their humanity to maintain this lifestyle while pretending everything is acceptable.

The transformative donor organizer's role includes helping wealthy people see how their own lives — and those of their families and future generations — will improve when systems of violence and domination are replaced with systems that center human life and dignity. When this understanding is deeply internalized, it can produce a lifelong commitment to fighting for a different world.

Developing Right Relationship to Power

The cumulative effect of personal transformation work can be summed up in what Solidaire's Political Education Strategist Chris Westcott has called "developing right relationship to power."

The concept of "right relationship" emerged from Indigenous communities and involves being in relationship with other people(s), as well as the land, air, water, plants, animals and past and future generations in ways that center sacredness, dignity, reciprocity, mutual responsibility, healing and sustainability. This way of being also includes repairing past harms and actions that have been out of alignment with these values.

So what does it mean to apply this concept of right relationship specifically to the exercise of power by wealthy people, most of whom are white?

Most wealthy people — especially those who are either white or belong to another dominant/ruling caste or ethnicity in their home culture — have been socialized to dominate others (often politely), to believe they are smarter and more competent than others and to seek and feel entitled to power over institutions and other people's lives.[23] When those behaviors are present, it takes a significant amount of time, trusted relationship and repetition to support real change.

Complicating this work is the fact that wealthy people (especially white people and inheritors) who self-select into progressive communities are often personally uncomfortable with their power. Those who have had more interaction with politicized working-class people, organizations and movements can actually come into donor organizing with a large amount of guilt and shame. When discomfort, guilt and shame are present, donors often act with the intention of taking up as little space as possible, rather than seeking to make positive contributions by using their power responsibly for liberatory ends.

Many progressive and Left donors have interacted with parts of Left movement, including people in leadership positions, that have communicated explicitly or implicitly that the correct way (especially for white people) to "be an ally" is to be very small, harshly call out other privileged people, feel guilty enough to give away a lot of money and try very hard not to hurt anyone.[24]

Wealthy people of color often face different dynamics. They can more easily "hide" their class identity in movement spaces, be accepted as comrades and even leaders and may be paternalistically assumed to have political clarity and class consciousness. Often, wealthy Black, Indigenous and people of color

---

23 Again, this is complicated by the fact that wealthy people's different family, race, class and gender experiences have shaped their socialization differently, but it is true that most of the wealthy people we organize either grew up in wealthy communities or have since been socialized through elite educational institutions and communities that intentionally instill owning-class culture and ways of relating to power. This class training is also very gendered — many wealthy women were socialized to rule or dominate in certain spaces, and over working-class women employees specifically, while being socialized to sublimate their own needs to the needs of men and children and to stay out of powerful roles and knowledge in male-dominated sectors like finance. For those who grew up working class and are entering these types of wealthy and powerful communities for the first time, their work toward a right relationship with power may actually need to focus more on navigating survivor's guilt and building an internal sense of agency and empowerment that is often damaged by internalized class, gender and/or race oppression.

24 My absolute favorite description of this is from Adam Roberts, who was a volunteer and staff leader in Resource Generation for many years: *"For a long time I thought the treatment for my white man-ness was to become more rigidly not-bad, something like the opposite of dancing"* ("Steven Returns to the Universe: If Grief Were a Weapon, What Shape Would It Take?," *Guernica*, March 21, 2022, https://www.guernicamag.com /steven-returns-the-universe).

donors are "let off the hook" for their excess wealth and power in a way that stifles their transformative leadership ability and impedes a deeper alignment with movements. Alternatively, once they start having a certain type of movement visibility or leadership, their class experience becomes used as one of many weapons to tear them down.

To create grounded wealthy leaders for liberation, we need to have practices that address both under-accountability and over-accountability around power and wealth, and help people land in a place of centered accountability. Under-accountability around wealth and power shows up as hoarding power or resources, being defensive, avoiding learning or avoiding responsibility, making excuses, engaging in denial or dishonesty, prioritizing individualism, not seeking input from or sharing power with movements, being self-righteous, acting with inconsistency or flakiness and downplaying or minimizing one's impact on others.

Over-accountability for wealth and power usually includes feeling shame (the sense of being inherently bad, unworthy, not good enough, harmful or not belonging) and therefore seeking to impact others as little as possible, hiding from power or resources, never taking risks or stepping into leadership, collapsing in response to mistakes or feedback, having intense anxiety, being silent or quiet, constantly apologizing, needing a lot of reassurance and avoiding people or tasks that make one face their identity, wealth and power. Over-accountability can also look like rushing to redistribute wealth in ways that don't account for the legitimate needs of oneself and one's family and that end up being self-punishing.

It's helpful to think of this as a pendulum on which people can swing easily from one side to the other. One example of a swing that happens regularly is that people give massive resources based on shame, guilt and outside pressure, and then suddenly retract from their giving — perhaps even not following through on pledges or committed gifts — and pull back from community.

Both of these extremes make it very difficult to be in a close or honest relationship, let alone to actually hold someone accountable to their commitments and values. The goal is to find a place of dynamic equilibrium somewhere in the center of the pendulum. Real accountability is both rigorous and compassionate.

For people with wealth and power, centered accountability is a balance of being thoughtful about positionality and taking risks in service of our highest values and our highest calling for justice. It requires developing one's own political compass and sense of integrity with one's own liberatory values and developing relationships of accountability with organizations led by working-class communities and communities of color. It is being authentic, actively seeking feedback, seeking to have a positive impact on others, being humble, being honest, acting with dignity, cultivating self-worth, being open, seeking connection, giving and receiving care, having the flexibility/will to change and being willing to make mistakes, get in conflicts, learn, repair and stay in relationship and community through them. Transformative Donor Organizing must support people to live in this centered accountability place as much as possible.

As Solidaire Donor Organizing Strategist Nigel Charles says, this work "actually requires a political vision that we are being organized into that moves us out of this dichotomy of 'am I a good person or am I a bad person,' which is not actually all that helpful, and it can shift us into a place of 'am I helping to bring this vision of the world into being?'"[25]

Healing Trauma and Countering Internalized Oppression and Superiority

Healing trauma is essential because unresolved trauma often drives the very behaviors that maintain wealth hoarding and separation from others — the fear, disconnection and need for control that keep wealthy people from fully engaging in justice work. When wealthy people heal their trauma, they can

---

25 Nigel Charles, interviewed by Michael Gast and Isaac Lev Szmonko, July 10, 2024.

move beyond survival-based thinking and develop the emotional capacity for genuine relationship-building, risk-taking and sustained commitment to collective liberation.

Trauma healing is specialized work that usually requires therapeutic support and/or cultural healing practices beyond what an organization can provide. However, transformative donor organizers must be able to recognize and understand the trauma and internalized oppression that wealthy people carry without taking on the role of healer or trying to solve these issues themselves.

What are examples of the complex intersection of internalized oppression and wealth that can show up in this process of transformation?

- In Solidaire, there are several women who grew up poor or working-class and then married into wealth, and need to do transformative work to come into their own sense of power around money and wealth redistribution.

- There are wealthy people of color whose families escaped war or other severe repression. Supporting these members to dig into their shared experience with other oppressed people and the ways wealth buffered them from certain consequences can create powerful, lifelong commitment to funding movements.

- And broadly, many wealthy women and queer people face patriarchal barriers to wealth redistribution because their full power is being blocked both by internalized sexism and by powerful men — usually husbands, fathers and financial advisors.

FIVE

Methodology: How Transformation Happens

Like every human, wealthy people need to be a part of organizations that care about them as whole people, about their personal struggles and triumphs, about what brings them to this work and where they need to grow and change. They need to be in organizations that believe in their capacity to transform and be powerful leaders in service of their politics, vision and values.

S everal reliable practices support transformation in donor organizing:

1. **Creating a community of belonging and practice** that consciously supports new ways of being.

2. **Facilitating personal revelation and discovery.** This work creates cracks in our fixed sense of self, opening space for embodied change. In the Transformative Donor Organizing model, political education should be centered around creating these kinds of openings in ways that are deeply politically rooted.

3. **Speaking the unspoken and unspeakable.** Domination requires shame, which causes hiding and inaction, and class is a place of near endless shame in American society. Transformation means bringing these hidden aspects into trusted groups that respond with compassion. Shame causes people to hide, thrives where things are hidden and, for most of us, is a place of deep stuckness and inaction that is a reliable block to acting in alignment with our otherwise deeply held values. Shame can actually cause us to act against our values. Transforming a shame mindset requires bringing things forth from the shadows into groups of trusted people who share some of the experience and can greet it with deep compassion.

4. **Building loving relationships across identities and experiences of power and oppression.** One of the fastest and deepest ways we see people transform is by entering into loving relationships with people who face different types of oppression than they personally do, whose suffering and resistance they then witness. While "personal" forms of love, like familial or romantic relationships, are often how people come to this change, the Transformative Donor Organizing model should seek ways to create loving relationships that cross differences and are beneficial for the transformation of people on both sides.

5. **Supporting protagonism and purpose**. Transformative Donor Organizing helps wealthy people experience the joy, pride, fulfillment and freedom of becoming agents of change, making meaningful contributions, living with a sense of personal integrity and finding purpose in creating a new world.

The following sections address key methods for transforming wealthy people into committed parts of Left movements who will redistribute their resources, lead others to do so and leverage their power for liberation.

Creating Political Home: "Organization Means Commitment" [26]

Everything in organizing centers on the belief that people need to belong in organizations to grow, develop as leaders and exercise collective power strategically. This is not how the Left typically treats its wealthy donors.

Transformative Donor Organizing requires wealthy people to have a long-term political home aligned with broader movements. This home should explicitly seek radical structural change: ending racial capitalism, imperialism, heteropatriarchy and colonization, and building socialism with democratic tendencies.

A political home provides:

1. **A counterbalance to individualism**. Everyone in America is indoctrinated into individualism. Those higher on the class and race ladder more intensely internalize it, especially if they haven't been forced

---

26 *Organization Means Commitment* (2011) is a pamphlet that was written by Grace Lee Boggs in the early 1970s, laying out her theories of what kind of revolutionary organizations were needed. It includes many of the foundational ideas that were incorporated into the Transformative Organizing model. In her introduction to the pamphlet in 2011, she wrote, "*Organization Means Commitment* was written to project a very different concept of revolutionary organization and leadership, the kind that could only be developed by many years of patient and protracted theoretical and practical struggles. ... To make a revolution people must not only struggle against existing institutions. They must make a philosophical leap and become more human human beings. In order to change/transform the world, they must change/transform themselves."

to rely on collective care for survival in the same way that working-class communities, immigrant communities and communities of color are often forced to operate to survive.[27] From the top of the wealth ladder, it is easier to firmly believe in the idea of meritocracy.

2. **Belonging and community**. Progressive wealthy people often feel they don't fully belong anywhere. Their wealthy families generally don't share their politics, and their progressive communities don't share their wealth. Many progressive wealthy people hide their wealth from activist communities for fear of judgment. If they don't have wealthy families, the alienation can be even deeper, and this is often amplified for wealthy people of color. Many wealthy people have also experienced emotional and financial abuse from their families — for example, access to money is used to control, manipulate and punish and/or they come into their wealth through the death of a loved one. This lived experience is often unacknowledged and very painful for many people. Finding community with others who have similar experiences and take this pain seriously can be a deeply healing experience.

3. **Connection to humanity**. Being rich in a violently unequal society is inherently a separating experience from almost everyone on the planet.[28] This separateness and alienation is exacerbated by the ways that wealthy people are socialized to feel a false sense of material scarcity. Owning-class culture teaches wealthy people to feel afraid and suspicious that everyone is going to come for their wealth, that people are only interested in relationships with them because of their wealth and that they should therefore a) accumulate as much wealth as possible, or at least not give

27 Nicole M. Stephens and Sarah Townsend, "Research: How You Feel About Individualism Is Influenced by Your Social Class," *Harvard Business Review,* May 22, 2017, https://hbr.org/2017/05/research-how-you-feel-about-individualism-is-influenced-by-your-social-class.

28 For those who are first-generation wealthy and for wealthy people of color, this feeling of separation can be particularly intimate — with difference from family and community of origin feeling acute and painful, even as they may be held up as an example of "success."

it away,[29] b) keep their wealth hidden, c) live and socialize only among other wealthy people who don't need their money and d) hide behind both bureaucratic and militarized violence that will keep other people away from their wealth.[30]

While the primary harm of this is clearly to the communities from which that wealth is extracted, this reality also causes psychological and spiritual harm to wealthy people.

Having a place to practice belonging is necessary to enter into the type of vulnerability that is required for transformation and provides a cushion for the pain that emerges when truly facing where wealth comes from (more on this below).[31] Whether or not wealthy people can always *feel* belonging, the organization should actively cultivate a positive culture of belonging through community-building, positive affirmation and recognition, responsiveness, appropriate affection and, where possible, one-on-one attention. Donor organizers will have more success if they can genuinely show that they like the wealthy people they are organizing. This is not easy, especially when staff or other leaders are being treated in classist, racist and sexist ways, but you can't effectively organize someone who can tell that you don't like them.

In a political home employing Transformative Donor Organizing, wealthy people have space to safely, vulnerably and bravely share both their experiences being on the receiving end of domination in relation to their wealth (i.e., from

---

29   Iris Brilliant's article "How the Wealthy White Family Forbids Wealth Redistribution" is a helpful deep dive on this dynamic within wealthy white families specifically (*Medium,* September 7, 2023, https://medium.com/@ iris_brilliant/how-the-wealthy-white-family-forbids-wealth-redistribution-10e6c5c06483).

30   This socialization is much deeper in people who were raised in wealthy families. However, pieces of it can be true for people who transition classes into wealth, especially when they start belonging to wealthy communities through elite institutions that are major purveyors of this culture and ideology. Additionally, the experience of suddenly being the only people in their community with wealth (and having lots of people who seek their financial support, including those they don't have genuine relationships with) can be an objectifying, alienating and fearful experience that produces similar needs but also requires specific community with other wealthy people who share those specific experiences, such as feeling very proud of becoming wealthy or having survivor's guilt.

31   I say "practice belonging" instead of "feel belonging" because in my experience, wealthy people really struggle with a sense of belonging and benefit from being told that they belong.

the humiliation, control and manipulation of parents or husbands) and any shame or dissociation they carry from having unearned power and privilege. Wealthy members are supported to share details about their wealth (like how much they have and where it came from) and notice any ways they are hiding or secretive about the money in their control.

The Transformative Donor Organizing model must create spaces for deeper trust and vulnerability for this kind of sharing and then support people to move into action that can create pride and dignity to replace the shame. Organizers must move from a place of understanding and respecting that it is courageous to be public about having wealth, to leverage personal relationships in support of movements, and to radically redistribute wealth when everything in one's family and home cultures says to keep accumulating.

This sense of belonging is particularly important when a wealthy person makes mistakes or faces bumps along the road. The marker of actual transformation is whether people retreat into old, dominant ways of wielding wealth and power when they face real challenges. Often, we see wealthy people renege on commitments, step out of movements or stop making progress after they endure certain types of family pressure, after they've made visible mistakes, after they've been treated poorly (or even just been given very direct feedback) by people with less positional power or when the overall political tide starts to shift from a visible movement moment back into long-term organizing and retrenchment. These are the times we need to do our best to pull people closer, but that works only if they already have the kinds of relationships that can bring them back in.

Cultivating belonging is central to the Transformative Donor Organizing approach. Like every human, wealthy people need to be a part of organizations that care about them as whole people, about their personal struggles and triumphs, about what brings them to this work and about where they need to grow and change. They need to be in organizations that believe in their capacity to transform and be powerful leaders in service of their politics, vision and values. In these settings, they can both grow into their bravest and most impactful selves and be "kept in" when things get hard.

Love and Spirit

Love is central to Transformative Donor Organizing. There are three quotes that elucidate the type of love we mean:

> *"Transformative organizing involves doing the work of loving each other in ways that seem ridiculous if we only think of revolutionary change as masses of people mobilized to make demands on a state. ... Even if we protest so effectively that we acquire state power, if we don't change our ways of thinking and relating to one another, we will only further develop this contradiction with new people in charge. These changes must be rooted in love.*
>
> *Because the next American Revolution must resolve this contradiction, the organizing that creates it will not simply be anti-imperialist, anti-racist, anti-sexist, or anti-ableist. ... The only way to secure freedom from these forms of oppression is to create the freedom to develop and practice new types of more human relationships. Only by developing these kinds of loving relationships can we as humans heal ourselves — and each other — from the damage done to us by an economic and political system bent on creating wealth at the expense of all living things."*
>
> — Grace Lee Boggs, *Organization Means Commitment*

> *"Love is an action, never simply a feeling. It is a combination of care, commitment, trust, knowledge, responsibility, and respect."*
>
> — bell hooks, *Communion: The Female Search for Love*

> *"Love cannot be sentimental. ... It must generate other acts of freedom; otherwise, it is not love."*
>
> — Paulo Freire, *Pedagogy of the Oppressed*

Solidaire actively brings love to our organizing practice and culture. This is a fundamental part of the culture that creates the conditions for transformation. We approach our members as whole humans who are a part of our beloved community. We see them in their dignity and their vulnerability, in their power and their growth edges. Love is not a feeling. It is the practice of recognizing the humanity of our members and standing with them in their struggle to embody their truest values and be their best versions of self. We do this with deep care and kindness.

For wealthy people, expanding the circle of love is a multifaceted project. Wealthy people usually need to learn to unconditionally love themselves and other wealthy people. This is a core part of learning how to do wealth redistribution and donor organizing work from a deep commitment to collective liberation, instead of from a place of shame. Similarly, wealthy people must learn to expand their circle of love to working-class communities, beyond charity or paternalism. As Omar El Akkad writes in *One Day, Everyone Will Have Always Been Against This* (2025), his book about the genocide in Gaza, "It may seem now like it's someone else's children, but there's no such thing as someone else's children."

A crucial part of Transformative Donor Organizing is helping people find a place of "calling" in the work. To be the most powerful agents of change we can, we need to transcend just thinking that this work is strategic and needs to be done, and seek and cultivate a feeling of sacred purpose, which can be felt by those around us.

Most spiritual, religious and humanist lineages value the righteousness of participating in healing or repairing the world and helping to provide for the well-being of all people. Whether or not we identify with the lineages of our ancestors, we can cultivate a shared sense of this deeper purpose of taking something fractured and doing our sacred part to make it whole.

Solidaire also infuses "spirit work" deeply into our organizing culture and practice. Ritual, meditation, deep reflection, prayer, ceremony, the calling in of energies, the development of a relationship to land and nature, griefletting and the cultivation of a sense of magic, awe and holiness or sacredness can all be powerful tools in Transformative Donor Organizing that instill commitment and purpose to building a new world.

Transformative Political Education: Creating the Cracks

Rigorous political education about history; racial capitalism and patriarchy; and Left organizing, strategy and vision is crucial to Transformative Donor Organizing but insufficient on its own. Movements often carry a false assumption that this type of political education with wealthy people automatically leads to aligned action or sustained commitment.

As Nigel Charles says, "Political education has to serve a purpose. Outside of the purpose, it's just watching a documentary — it's nice; it's a good brain exercise. But I think particularly with donor organizing, it has to help wealthy people better see their own positionality — the ways that the system is benefiting them, propping them up, giving them disproportionate access to power. And then how to actually navigate in a way that is different."[32] As we mentioned above, it's also important for wealthy people to see how the current system is harmful not only to others, but also to themselves.

Like all effective political education, methodology matters. Because of their experiences with higher education, many wealthy people have a higher-than-average tolerance for didactic or lecture-style education. They can listen intently, take notes and regurgitate what you've taught them — but it won't necessarily change anything about their behavior.

We've found that several components to education are necessary to make change possible:

1. **Create a group atmosphere that centers belonging.** Solidaire members constantly tell us that they are concerned they won't belong in a space we're leading — because they don't have enough money, or have too much money or don't know enough, etc. Relationship-building and an intentionally affirmative culture that values each person's contributions

---

32   Interview with Michael Gast and Isaac Lev Szmonko, July 10, 2024.

are core to creating an atmosphere where people can relax into belonging and then be braver and more honest. It's important to invite everyone's voices in the room as early and often as possible, and to include lots of opportunities to connect deeply and personally in pairs or small groups.

2. **Prioritize personal storytelling and self-discovery.** Wealthy people need opportunities to share their own stories and how they relate to the subject matter — whether that's what they were taught about money growing up, how they're still struggling not to embody classism in their giving, how their family's history interacts with the history of anti-Black racism in this country or how patriarchy impacts their family giving. Social justice movements often (rightfully) center the experiences of working-class communities and communities of color in political education. While it's important for wealthy people to (learn how to) do that, relating to this subject matter personally is also crucial to creating deeper engagement and change. Donor organizations are generally the only places where people can share these types of stories in politicized and politicizing ways.

3. **Engage in open-ended inquiry.** It is tempting with privileged populations to revert to questions with right answers or simply tell them what the right answer is: Think this. Do this. Sometimes, this type of guidance is genuinely helpful, as it can be when learning the specific ways to give to movements that reduce harmful powerful dynamics. However, open-ended questions requiring personal and critical thinking should be central to any transformative political education.

4. **Feature embodied learning.** Somatic practices, family conversation role-plays, electoral organizing, politicized rituals — finding ways for wealthy people to get out of their heads and into their hearts, bodies and spirits is crucial for creating behavioral change. As a general rule, this population has been constantly rewarded for "being smart" in ways that are deeply disembodied and grounded in Western, white supremacist and patriarchal culture.

Creating an Understanding of Where the Money Really Comes From

Helping wealthy people develop a specific and politicized understanding of where their wealth comes from is a primary way to create a sustained commitment to acting in alignment with liberation movements.

While wealthy people often arrive to progressive donor networks feeling that wealth inequality is bad, very few wealthy people come with an understanding of how wealth is accumulated in our society and how their specific wealth was accumulated vis-à-vis racial capitalism. It takes study and support to learn how the engines of economic development and wealth accumulation in Europe and the Americas were colonization, genocide, slavery, imperialism, patriarchy and labor exploitation, and how those forces continue today. It takes sustained attention to learn about those systems and how they connect with one's personal and family lineage.

The study involved and support needed look different, depending on where the wealth came from.

For white inheritors who discover their families' direct connections to slavery, genocide, war or exploitative industries, this information can create a deep desire for repair and wealth return. For those with newer wealth, including many people of color with wealth, understanding how real estate and stock market wealth connect to racial capitalism can be an essential motivator.

Addressing Blind Spots: A Detailed Description of Transformative Donor Organizing Political Education

For Solidaire members whose wealth comes from businesses or real estate, it's important to develop an understanding of the real sources of their wealth: property values driven by structural racism and business profits extracted from workers and land — all backed by state power and violence.

For Solidaire members who became rich through investments in the stock market, it's important to provide chances to learn:

- Where their money is invested[33]

- How stock market profits are actually made through resource extraction and the exploitation of people, which are always facilitated by violence

- How because of the history and structures of our political economy, this extraction and exploitation especially harms people of color, poor women and people in the Global South to make the global owning class rich

- How financialization hides and abstracts this violence

- Alternative ways to invest money into regenerative economies that build collective resources for poor and working-class communities and communities of color in sustainable ways

Here is an example of the political education possible by looking closer at an investment portfolio and our economy:

> If a wealthy person is invested in tech stocks, they are actually invested in many harmful processes, including near-slavery-like conditions in the Congo, where the cobalt for rechargeable batteries is being mined and poor Black people die to extract it. These conditions exist because of coercive international trade agreements between the US and the Congo, which are possible because of the history of Belgian colonization and ongoing imperialist domination by the US-led World Bank and International Monetary Fund, which holds the Congolese in unpayable debt for "borrowing" from the countries that stole wealth and people from them.
>
> The technology supply chain further relies on poorly paid workers in Southeast Asia who assemble components in dangerous conditions. This entire system runs through shipping networks established during the slave trade and maintained through military power and fossil fuels. The products are then sold by minimum wage workers while CEOs and

---

33 This can often be harder than it might at first seem, given the diversification of portfolios and situations in which people are invested in blended stock indexes that hide the specific companies and industries being invested in.

shareholders get rich. Additionally, these technology companies often profit from government contracts to provide surveillance technology to aid in war and policing.

A wealthy person who fails to recognize these connections may view wealth accumulation as passive or neutral, rather than acknowledging its active role in perpetuating harm. They may think, "It's better that I keep accumulating this money so that I can give more over time," without realizing they are extracting wealth from the very communities they are hoping to support.

Importantly, this type of political education must help people place their wealth within a systemic context, understanding this whole chain of exploitation and oppression, so the answer isn't just personal divestment. We must help them reach the conclusion: "We need systemic solutions for systemic problems. We need to work together with working-class people to transform these harmful systems. My personal giving is important but not enough. I can give up any quest for salvation or righteousness and join with others in making a better world."

We want wealthy people to move from asking questions oriented toward their own purity, righteousness or moral salvation to asking, "What are the strategic roles I can play to fight, dismantle and transform the structures that currently exist? How can I and we best support the people who are most targeted by those systems to lead those struggles?"

We want it to be clear that moving money to grassroots organizing is one of the most strategic ways that wealthy people can contribute to this work for structural change. And we want to help our members understand that the money they donate today is a small fraction of what they can influence or move if they become a lifelong peer organizer and fundraiser.

In the Transformative Donor Organizing approach, political education seeks to support wealthy people to take on one of the most strategic roles they can play in movement: to organize other wealthy people and philanthropic institutions to align with and support grassroots movements.

Collective Action and Participation in Movements Led by Working-Class People of Color

When movements are very present in the streets and in the news, many progressive wealth holders move toward social justice movements for the first time. Solidaire experienced this particular type of surge of new members during the resistance to the first Trump administration and during the Black-led uprisings against police violence in 2014 and 2020. When wealthy and white people witness mass leadership from communities of color, it can accelerate transformation dramatically. Witnessing liberatory collective power creates embodied understanding that another world is possible and worth everything.

While witnessing movement moments provides important entry points, the transformative power of *participating* in liberatory movements led by working-class people of color cannot be overstated. Many Solidaire members who enter donor networks are already involved with such movements, while for others, these networks provide their first exposure.

For this reason, it's important for Left donor organizations to provide opportunities to both learn from such movements and take action with them when that's appropriate.

Here are examples of how Solidaire has supported this type of engagement:

1. A contingent of Solaire members went to Minnesota to join the Indigenous-led movement Stop Line 3, targeting a harmful oil pipeline.

2. Mobilized members took part in Christians for a Free Palestine actions to pressure legislators to cut off US military aid to Israel.

3. Solidaire Action organized members to knock on doors with groups that build electoral power in working-class communities of color with Seed the Vote.

Beyond learning, there is a transformative cultural vibrancy and sense of political power that many wealthy people, especially wealthy white people, experience for the first time through actions like this. Feeling a sense of belonging to collective power across difference is irreplaceable.

Leadership Development: Moving From Passive Allyship to Protagonism and Strategic Leadership

Leadership development is a core part of all Transformative Organizing and is part of Solidaire's 10-Year Strategy: "unleashing donor and investor protagonism in movement building."[34]

Transformative Donor Organizing posits that we need to turn as many owning-class people we can into leaders and organizers for wealth and power redistribution, as a part of movements led by working-class people of color for revolutionary structural change.

Strong donor organizing leaders share core characteristics and capacities:

- Political alignment with both liberatory vision and the organization's strategy and purpose

- Belief in wealthy people's abilities to transform

- Doing their best to practice what they preach with their own giving, investing, organizing, and advocacy

- Ability to build trusting relationships, including with wealthy people who are very different from them and/or at a different stage of their personal and political development

- Being able to ask questions and listen for what's under the surface with curiosity and compassion, particularly when wealthy people are stuck or acting out of alignment with their values

---

34 *10-Year Strategy* (Solidaire 2023).

- Giving direct feedback kindly

- Assessing and inviting people into the next brave step in their leadership

- Speaking about their own wealth, politics and values in ways that are accessible and relatable, beyond preaching to the choir

- Training in relational fundraising, so that they are equipped to move resources beyond their own

- Developing other leaders with these core capacities

In the Transformative Donor Organizing model, leadership development involves both building these capacities and creating opportunities for members to exercise them. A Transformative Donor Organizing organization needs to provide places for people to practice new skills in a safe and supported environment as part of building their overall confidence and ability to take risks for the sake of our shared political aspirations.

Again, this requires supporting people to passionately align their lives with liberatory movements, not just their money. If wealthy people see themselves as a part of a broader community whose sacred work is to radically change the world, and believe that their own long-term interests are in that new world, then they are able to more consistently align their lives and actions to make that vision a reality.

Moving people from the relative passivity of being a donor into their full protagonism requires regularly building up people's confidence by celebrating them and supporting them to believe that they are/can be powerful agents for change. As Nigel Charles pointed out, this work requires honoring people's dignity and really being able to see, uplift and develop the specific gifts they bring.

There are **several key roadblocks** to supporting wealthy people to become liberatory leaders that must be addressed through political education and leadership development.

1. **A service orientation toward wealthy people**. Our political, economic and social systems are built to maintain and grow rich people's

wealth, while instilling in people across class the idea that wealthy and powerful people earned their positions of power by being better than everyone else. Materially and culturally, we are set up to either be wealthy people or to serve wealthy people. Wealthy people are trained to expect service and deference. This power dynamic is often invisible to the owning class but defines the reality of everyone else. Meanwhile, poor, working-class and middle-class people are taught — explicitly and implicitly — that failure to serve well can bring punishment: losing jobs, housing, children, stability or access to basic needs. Unfortunately, lots of donor organizing spaces replicate these dynamics. Transformative Donor Organizing must walk a fine and sometimes blurry line of supporting wealthy people while refusing to "serve" them, instead staying in service of broader working-class-led movements. This balance requires building relationships centered in care and compassion, while having an orientation toward truth-telling, regularly naming and intervening in harmful power dynamics or ways of being, and being willing to sometimes hurt wealthy people's feelings in the process. In our experience, doing this skillfully actually builds trust and commitment instead of unnecessarily pushing wealthy people away. We need to move away from the dominant tendencies to either coddle or punish wealthy people and care about them enough to be invested in their real growth.

2. **Mixed messaging about power**. On the one hand, owning-class people have generally been taught to use power in excessive, dominating, irresponsible and unaccountable ways. But then they enter into movements in which many people feel like leadership is bad, power is bad and power among wealthy people and white people is particularly and inherently bad and shouldn't ever be used. As transformative organizers, we need to deal with both sides of that harmful messaging. We must support wealthy people to learn how to share power and to use their power in direct alignment, accountability and collaboration with liberatory movements.

3. **Positionality barriers**. Leaders will face unique challenges based on their specific backgrounds and points of entry into this work:

   a. Wealthy members who grew up working class often need specific support owning their new class experience enough to have confidence and compassion in relating to people who were raised with wealth. Similarly to those who were raised working class and still are, these folks may require support overcoming internalized classist, racist and sexist messaging to see themselves as leaders.

   b. Wealthy people who joined working-class-centered movements before they got politicized around (or came into) their wealth often still relate to their wealth experience with shame or distancing. This often means they haven't actually done (grounded, strategic) wealth redistribution and/or that they relate to people with shared race/class experiences who are less politically developed with self-righteousness or just plain ineffectiveness.

Politicized, Practical and Personalized Support Around Giving, Investing and Family/Community Organizing

The bureaucratic structures, family cultures and professional services that deal with wealth are set up to automatically support wealthy people to get richer. Billions of dollars are spent this way. This is sometimes referred to as the wealth defense industry, and it's deeply ingrained in owning class culture.[35]

---

35 "Owning class culture" refers to the shared values, behaviors and worldview of people whose wealth comes primarily from ownership of capital rather than labor. This culture typically emphasizes individual achievement over collective well-being, views wealth accumulation as natural and deserved and prioritizes maintaining control and social distance through exclusive institutions and indirect communication styles. Key characteristics include comfort with extreme inequality, preference for charity over systemic change, conflict avoidance and expectation of deference from others.

Every wealthy person has multiple people paid directly (and millions indirectly) to defend and grow their wealth.

In the face of this onslaught, wealthy people will always need one-on-one support to move against these dominant forces. Even when a wealthy person wants to move their money or leverage their power, the actual mechanics are often quite complex and the resistance is almost always significant.

Given this reality, we must offer individualized support in several key areas:

Understanding Assets and Right-Sizing Giving Capacity

When wealthy people try to apply their Left political values to their own lives, one of the primary questions that arises is *How much is enough money to keep for themselves and their families, and how much should they give away?* There are several complicated problems that arise with this question that Transformative Donor Organizing should seek to help people resolve:

1. Wealthy people's perspective on how much money they need is fundamentally skewed by the fact that they are accustomed to living on an amount of money based on severe inequality and material excess. Even models that say something like, "When you retire you should have 25 years of your living expenses" don't account for the fact that wealthy people's annual living expenses are usually outsized compared to your average person, and that wealthy people are trained to compare up and consider themselves not very wealthy if they aren't billionaires.[36]

2. Many wealthy people who inherited money earlier in their lives have never earned enough money through work to meet their living expenses, and some have not even earned enough to meet a much more modest set of living expenses. This lack of experience creates a lack of confidence that they can sustain themselves financially through work, as well as a

---

36   Michael Gast, "Always Compare Up," *Organize the Rich*, April 29, 2014, https://organizetherich.substack.com/p /always-compare-up.

reluctance to do that if they don't have to. All of this makes people want to hold on to much more money.

3. Many wealthy people are raised to assume that things like safety, security and stability can only come from vast sums of money, as opposed to being in a web of loving relationships and a larger community that has your back.

4. Generally, the only professional support for answering the question of *How much is enough?* comes from wealth managers who have a personal financial stake in their clients accumulating more wealth, and who also operate under an idea of how much money people should have to retire that is based on numbers very few people will attain.[37]

5. The answer to the question of how much wealth to keep is different if you are 24, able-bodied and have multigenerational wealth; if you are first-generation wealthy and financially support a dozen family members in your home country who are poor; or if you are retired or disabled in a way that prevents you from earning money through work. It's not uncommon for young inheritors to decide not to give away millions of dollars because they think they will need it for retirement, even though they theoretically have 40-50 years they could work and save, and most will inherit way more resources in the future when their parents pass.

Left donor organizers need to learn how to support wealthy people in navigating these questions in a way that helps people move through a false sense of scarcity by both dealing with the real emotional blocks and politically situating their financial reality with other people's financial realities.

---

37 Our members are often advised to keep multiple millions of dollars for retirement. According to Vanguard, the median 401(k) savings for a 65-year-old in the US in 2023 was just $88,488, and the Employee Benefit Research Institute says that only 3.2% of Americans have $1 million or more in their retirement accounts: *How America Saves 2024* (Vanguard, 2024), https://corporate.vanguard.com/content/dam/corp/research/pdf/how_america_saves_report_2024.pdf; Chris Neiger, "How Many People Really Save $1 Million for Retirement?," *Motley Fool Money*, November 20, 2024, https://www.fool.com/money/buying-stocks/articles/how-many-people-really-save-1-million-for-retirement/#:~:text=You%27re%20not%20alone,in%20their%20retirement%20accounts.

We also need more aligned money coaches who can work with individuals and families, and professional financial advisors who will support wealthy people to end their dependence on inherited and excess wealth and redistribute boldly in their lifetimes, while still saving for retirement and emergencies. For those with inherited wealth, this can mean supporting them to figure out how to get well-paying jobs that cover their living expenses for the first time.

Creating Bold Multi-year Giving Plans

Wealthy people need to learn how to give their money strategically to frontline, grassroots movements without needing to become personal experts on the entire US and international Left (or even whatever sectors they most want to fund). Multi-year giving plans are the most reliable means to help wealthy people give proactively, substantively and strategically.

When donor networks seek to educate and transform people, but then don't support them to make giving plans, fewer dollars move and what money does move often goes to "false solutions," grasstops work or whoever has the best communications and major donor fundraising program. The current ways donor networks have tried to solve this problem (outside of helping their members create giving plans) include 1) offering their members a lot of political education and hoping their members give in alignment with what they learn, 2) establishing or uplifting aligned regranting institutions or pooled funds, 3) advising donors directly on places to give or connecting people with external donor or philanthropic advisors for their personal or family giving and 4) having a set of steady or emergent organizational partners that members are asked to donate to directly.

Strategies 2 through 4 all have significant strengths and flaws but are important tools. With these tools, organizations doing donor organizing do not leave people at a precipice alone, to stall or make poor decisions at the exact moment when having expert-aligned decision-making could make the difference in their ability to move money confidently and strategically.

Having a giving plan is the most time-tested way for wealthy people to move from a reactive to a proactive place around their giving and be able to make multiyear general operating support commitments.

Transformative Giving Practices

Even the best intentioned donors need to be taught how to give in ways that actively intervene in harmful power dynamics between philanthropy and movement, and to support movements to thrive.

All transformative donor organizers should know how to support someone to evaluate their current giving/grantmaking practices and encourage people to reassess and make adjustments.

Having Left donor organizers who are also experienced fundraisers can be really helpful for talking in detail with wealthy members about the impact of their giving practices.

Such giving practices have been articulated many times by different groups in social justice philanthropy spaces since the 1970s, including RG's Social Justice Philanthropy Principles.[38] Solidaire has adapted our own version in the last year, which can be found online.[39]

Organizing Key Decision Makers

Many progressive wealthy people do not have complete control over the resources they are giving and must persuade others to either cede control of resources entirely or allow them to make specific gifts to movements.

It's helpful if Left donor organizers develop skills to support wealthy people who need to navigate difficult family dynamics to be able to move money. When access to wealth is specifically through family, people's childhood

---

38 "Social Justice Philanthropy Principles," Resource Generation, accessed August 4, 2025, https://bit.ly/sjphilan-thropyprinciples.

39 Solidaire, "Solidaire's Do's & Don'ts of Social Justice Giving," n.d., https://bit.ly/socialjusticegiving.

triggers and traumas often get in the way, creating "fight, flight or freeze" reactions and narrowing their vision.

Supporting wealth holders to navigate family dynamics with care and purpose is one of the primary skill sets needed to unlock much larger amounts of capital effectively. In addition, it's helpful to have referral lists of people who are politically aligned and skilled at facilitating different types of this work within families, using their skills in offering political education, managing family conflicts and political differences, advising on giving, establishing or dissolving a family giving vehicle and building direct connections with movement vehicles.

Divesting from the Stock Market and Investing in Movements

Once people are politicized around the harms of the stock market, it's easy to get them to *want* to move their invested money into movements, but many people require individualized support to navigate the many internal and external barriers that arise in the process.

Donor organizations would benefit from having some combination of 1) a referral list of relatively aligned investment managers; 2) a regularly updated list of movement or movement-aligned organizations that take direct investments, with clarity about terms; 3) in-house investment advising or direct investment opportunities and 4) language or other resources for basic screens that people can use when talking with their current investment managers about reducing the harm of their current investments.

Navigating the Wealth Defense Industry

Donors who want to do significant giving to social justice work routinely face obstructions from financial managers, accountants and tax attorneys who work for them or their families. Wealth managers, who are financially incentivized and legally bound to make their clients as much money as possible, regularly advise donors to give less money away, to give only tax-deductible gifts or to stay invested in harmful industries. Tax accountants and attorneys are generally paid to help clients avoid as many taxes as possible to keep money in the hands of the wealthy and away from the public good. Even with good intentions, very few real estate lawyers or realtors are equipped to skillfully navigate land transfer back to an Indigenous nation. And donors face many confusing technical and legal problems when trying to navigate the rules of trusts. Often, all of these situations are also laden with patriarchal dynamics.

Donor organizers should understand the regular challenges that people who are trying to move money face in this realm and be able to offer some basic knowledge of what others have done with those challenges and/or referrals to aligned donors or professionals who deal with them.

Philanthropic Campaigns with Transformative Demands

One of the tenets of the Transformative Organizing model is that it uses transformative, counter-hegemonic demands,[40] creating campaigns to shift meaningful power and resources toward working-class communities and communities of color, while shifting the narrative and culture that supports systems of exploitation.

Transformative Donor Organizing should seek to have donors participate in campaigns that strategically use their political connections in coordination with grassroots movements, make transformative demands on philanthropy and other parts of the wealth protection industry, redesign philanthropic institutions to shift meaningful power and resources to grassroots movements and disrupt common assumptions that uphold philanthropy as a place to preserve and protect wealthy people's power and money.

---

40 If hegemony is the set of ideas, beliefs and norms that the ruling class uses to persuade people to consent to their own domination, counter-hegemonic demands are those that intentionally break with those ways of thinking to attempt to create a new common sense — e.g., "Housing is a human right," as opposed to the dominant belief that the market should control access to housing, or a campaign for a universal basic income.

If the ultimate goal is to enact systemic wealth redistribution that creates multiracial, working-class-led governance structures, what are the short-, medium- and long-term demands we should make regarding wealth and philanthropy?

Here are examples of what people have tried and are trying:

- Raising taxes on the rich

- Changing the philanthropy rules that govern payout, transparency, tax deductions or donor-advised funds

- Shifting the power of decision-making to include movement leaders who organize working-class communities and communities of color

Conclusion: A Call to Strategic Wealth Redistribution

We can create political homes for wealthy people that balance deep belonging with rigorous accountability. We can support their transformation with unflinching political education and compassionate community. We can develop their leadership to organize more wealthy people. Through these efforts and meaningful relationships with grassroots movements, we can unleash unprecedented resources for working-class power-building.

This journey toward Transformative Donor Organizing isn't just about better fundraising. It's about fundamentally reshaping how we understand the role of wealth and wealthy people in movements for liberation. Traditional approaches are strategically insufficient for the world we need to build.

We can create political homes for wealthy people that balance deep belonging with rigorous accountability. We can support their transformation with unflinching political education and compassionate community. We can develop their leadership to organize more wealthy people. Through these efforts and meaningful relationships with grassroots movements, we can unleash unprecedented resources for working-class power-building.

The work of Transformative Donor Organizing is deeply strategic, complex and unavoidably messy. It refuses easy binaries of "good" versus "bad" wealthy people. Instead, it invites wealthy people into principled struggle with their relationship to power and privilege. This allows them to embrace their role in our collective liberation more fully.

By supporting wealthy people to move through shame into action, we build the cross-class solidarity needed for revolutionary struggle. This work is part of a broader ecosystem of organizing strategies. Together, these strategies give us our best chance at building the multiracial, democratic, feminist, socialist future our movements envision.

In a world of devastating inequality, authoritarianism and climate crisis, Transformative Donor Organizing has a vital purpose. It frees up maximum resources, relationships and leadership capacity from the owning class for liberatory struggle. At the same time, it supports wealthy people to find dignity, purpose and joy as a part of communities fighting to bring a new world into being.

If wealthy people see themselves as a part of a broader community whose sacred work is to radically change the world, and believe that their own long-term interests are in that new world, then they are able to more consistently align their lives and actions to make that vision a reality.

Acknowledgments

T he insights in this article emerge from years of collective work alongside organizers, donors and movement leaders who have dedicated themselves to building a more just world.

I have been particularly influenced by the Catalyst Project's and Resource Generation's approaches to organizing white and/or wealthy people for collective liberation. My understanding of Transformative Organizing has been shaped deeply by leaders from Right to the City Alliance, Grassroots Global Justice Alliance and LeftRoots, as well as Barbara Ransby's and Charles M. Payne's documentation of Ella Baker, the Student Nonviolent Coordinating Committee and other Black organizers in the civil rights struggle.

Thanks to my early readers, who gave crucial feedback on the ideas: Jes Kelley, Rajasvini Bhansali, Rachel Gelman, Willa Conway, Farhad Ebrahimi, Mijo Lee, Erin Heaney, Ava Bynum, Nora Leccese, Braeden Lentz, Bridget Brehen, Jessie Spector, MJ McClure and Alia Trindle. Thank you to Dawn Phillips, Cindy Wiesner and DrewChristopher Joy for feedback on the description of Transformative Organizing. A conversation with Nigel Charles particularly deepened my thinking. Anything good is because of them, and any mistakes are all mine.

Special thanks go to Michael Gast of Organize the Rich, who has been with me at every step of this journey — from teaching me how to organize wealthy people with love, as my first supervisor at Resource Generation, to helping me develop and work the ideas of this piece more deeply into Solidaire's organizing, to accompanying me on the writing retreat that birthed this, to project-managing me and doing so many hours of editing my run-on sentences and repetition. It really wouldn't have been possible without you.

Thank you to Cynthia Williams and Barni Qaasim for their careful copyediting and to Design Action Collective for bringing the report to life visually.